Hyena

by Grace Hansen

Abdo
AFRICAN ANIMALS
Kids

abdopublishing.com

Published by Abdo Kids, a division of ABDO, P.O. Box 398166, Minneapolis, Minnesota 55439.

Printed in the United States of America, North Mankato, Minnesota.

102017

012018

THIS BOOK CONTAINS
RECYCLED MATERIALS

Photo Credits: iStock, Shutterstock

Production Contributors: Teddy Borth, Jennie Forsberg, Grace Hansen

Design Contributors: Dorothy Toth, Laura Mitchell

Publisher's Cataloging in Publication Data

Names: Hansen, Grace, author.

Title: Hyena / by Grace Hansen.

Description: Minneapolis, Minnesota : Abdo Kids, 2018. | Series: African animals |
         Includes glossary, index and online resource (page 24).

Identifiers: LCCN 2017943132 | ISBN 9781532104190 (lib.bdg.) | ISBN 9781532105319 (ebook) |
         ISBN 9781532105876 (Read-to-me ebook)

Subjects: LCSH: Hyenas--Juvenile literature. | Hyaenidae--Juvenile literature. |
         Zoology--Africa--Juvenile literature.

Classification: DDC 599.743 --dc23

LC record available at https://lccn.loc.gov/2017943132

Table of Contents

Hyena Habitat

Hyenas live in Africa. Spotted hyenas are one of the most common species. They can be found throughout much of the continent.

4

Spotted hyenas live in groups called clans. Clans live in grasslands and woodlands. They live in swamps and savannas too.

Hyenas often rest in shade or water in the daytime. They are more active at night, when it is cooler.

Body

Spotted hyenas are covered in brown hair. They have dark spots on their bodies and faces.

10

Spotted hyenas are the largest hyena **species**. They can weigh up to 190 pounds (86.2 kg). Females are much bigger than males.

Food & Hunting

Hyenas are meat eaters. They hunt and scavenge. Hyenas will hunt alone or as a clan.

Lone hyenas commonly eat birds, small mammals, and insects. Clan hunts allow for bigger meals, like zebra.

17

Baby Hyenas

Females give birth to one or two cubs in a **den**. A cub weighs about 1 pound (0.5 kg) at birth. It has black fur.

18

Cubs drink their mothers' milk for about a year. The clan helps raise the cubs. It teaches the cubs to hunt.

More Facts

- Unlike many pack animals, female hyenas lead the group. They are larger and stronger than males.

- Hyenas can run for long periods of time without getting tired. They can reach speeds of 35 miles per hour (56 km/h)!

- Hyenas have large heads. Their jaws are powerful. They have one of the strongest bites of any mammal.

Glossary

den – a wild animal's home.

scavenge – to search for dead animals as food.

species – a group of animals that look alike and can produce young together.

Index

Abdo Kids
ONLINE
FREE! ONLINE MULTIMEDIA RESOURCES

Visit **abdokids.com** and use this code to access crafts, games, videos, and more!

Abdo Kids Code:
AHK4190